A to Z Animals

by Michael Kania

Say and trace each letter. Learn about each animal. Answer the question on each page!

First published by Experience Early Learning Co.
7243 Scotchwood Lane, Grawn, Michigan 49637 USA

Text copyright © 2016 by Experience Early Learning Co.
Printed and bound in the USA

ISBN 978-1-937954-34-5
Visit us at **www.ExperienceEarlyLearning.com**

Alligator babies hatch from eggs, and the temperature of their nest is important. A warmer nest produces boy alligators. A cooler nest produces girls.

A is for Alligator

Do you like warmer or cooler weather?

B is for Bird

Birds are the only animals that have feathers. (Feathers are made of the same stuff as your fingernails!)

If you were a bird, what color would your feathers be?

C is for Camel

Camels are made for the desert. Their wide feet keep them from sinking in the sand. They can close their nostrils to keep out sand. And they can travel for months without food or water!

What do you think the desert is like?

D is for Dolphin

Dolphins like to talk to each other. They squeak, whistle, slap their tails, leap out of the water, snap their jaws and even bump heads to communicate!

How can you communicate without using words?

E is for Elephant

An elephant's trunk can: smell (like your nose can), pick things up (like your hands can), reach and push things (like your arms can), drink water (like a straw can), and even help breathe underwater (like a snorkel can)!

If you had a trunk, what would you do with it?

F is for Fox

Foxes have whiskers on their legs as well as on their faces, which help them find their way.

What can you use to find your way?

G is for Gorilla

What if you had to build a new bed every night?

Gorillas sleep in nests. They make them on the ground or in trees. Gorillas build a new nest every night.

H is for Hippo

Hippos spend most of their day in the water. At dusk, they leave the water to find food (mostly grass). One hippo can eat up to 150 pounds of grass in one night!

How do you know when you are full?

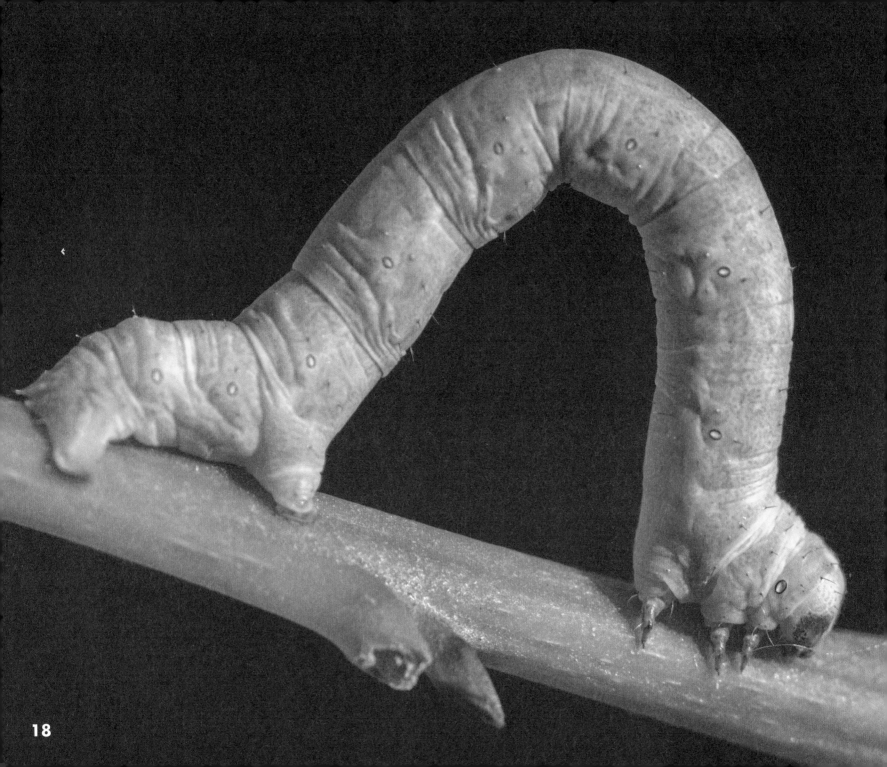

18

I is for Inchworm

Inchworms are named for the way they move. They stretch their front legs forward then pull their back legs up to meet the front ones, forming a loop in the middle. This special walk makes it look like inchworms are measuring their path, inch by inch.

What are some different ways that you can move?

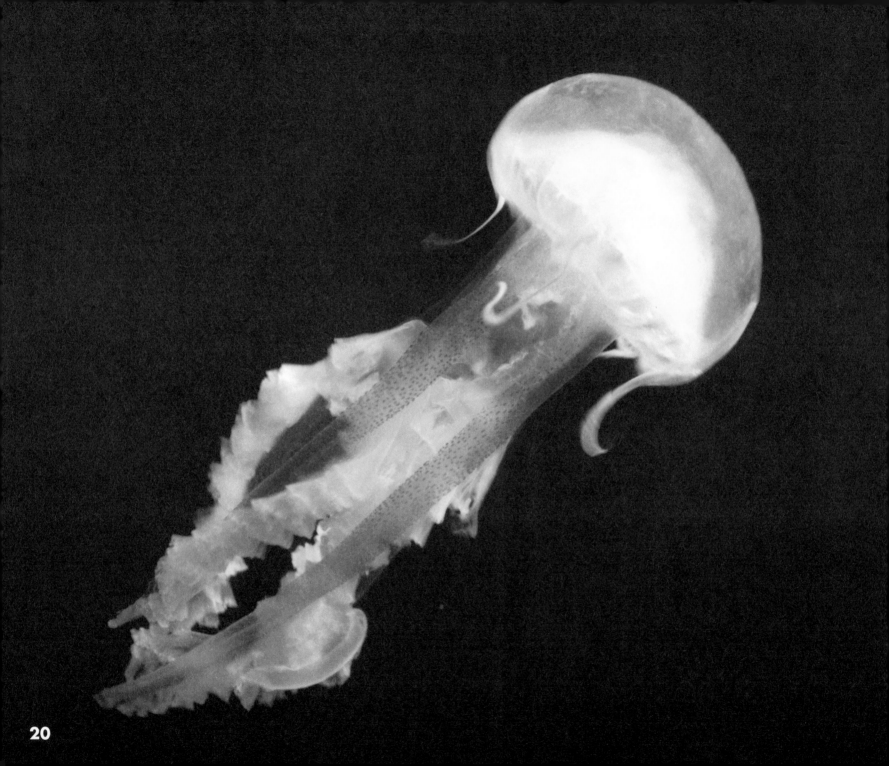

J is for
Jellyfish

Jellyfish do not have brains. They have a loose network of nerves in their skin that helps them sense changes in their environment.

What can you sense with your skin?

K is for
Kangaroo

A joey (baby kangaroo) is no
bigger than a grape when
it is born! It crawls into its
mother's pouch and stays
there for about 8 months
while it continues to grow.

How big were you
when you were born?

L is for
Llama

Llamas can carry heavy loads, but they will refuse to carry a load that is *too* heavy. They may lie down, hiss, spit, or kick, and they will not move until their load is lightened.

M is for Moose

At just five
days old,
a baby moose
can run
faster than
you can!

What can you do now that you couldn't do as a baby?

N is for
Newt

Newts can regrow
their body parts.
They can grow lost
legs, tails— even eyes!

What do you do when you are hurt?

O is for
Otter

Otters have very thick fur. It traps air to keep them warm in the water.

P is for Polar Bear

Polar bear fur looks white, but it is actually clear. Each hair is a hollow tube that holds heat from the sun.

What color is your hair?

Q is for Quail

When in danger, quail run away instead of flying. They can only fly for short distances, but they are fast runners and good at hiding.

How fast can you run?

R is for Rattlesnake

A rattlesnake's rattle is made up of hollow rings (made from the same stuff as your fingernails... and feathers!)

Each time a snake sheds its skin, a ring is added.

Can you count the rings on the snake's rattle?

37

S is for Sheep

Sheep have great memories. They can recognize the faces of other sheep (and people) and can remember them for years.

Whose faces do you know by heart?

T is for Tiger

Unlike other cats, tigers like the water. They are good swimmers.

Do you like to be in the water?

U is for Urchin

Sea urchins live for a long time. Most live for about 30 years, but the red urchin can live for over 200 years!

Who is the oldest person you know?

V is for Vulture

Vultures are the cleaners and trash collectors of the animal kingdom. They eat the leftovers from the hunts of other animals.

How do you help to keep your home clean?

W is for Wolf

Wolves live and hunt in packs. When pups (baby wolves) are born, they cannot see or hear. The whole pack helps to feed and care for them.

What are some things you do with your family?

X is for X-ray Fish

X-ray fish have skin
you can see through.
This helps the fish blend
in with plants and rocks
and makes it hard for
predators to catch them.

Y is for Yak

In the winter, a yak digs in the snow with its large horns to find plants to eat.

What tools do you use with your food?

Z is for
Zebra

A zebra's ears can tell you about its mood. Upright means "relaxed," pulled back means "angry," and pushed forward means "frightened."

What are clues you can see that tell you how your friend is feeling?